Thirty-One Questions on
Adoration of
the Blessed Sacrament

Thirty-One Questions on Adoration of the Blessed Sacrament

A Resource of the Bishops' Committee on the Liturgy

PASTORAL LITURGY SERIES • **TWO**

BISHOPS' COMMITTEE ON THE LITURGY
UNITED STATES CONFERENCE OF CATHOLIC BISHOPS
Washington, D.C.

The document *Thirty-One Questions on Adoration of the Blessed Sacrament* was developed as a resource by the Bishops' Committee on the Liturgy of the United States Conference of Catholic Bishops (USCCB). It was reviewed by the committee chairman, Cardinal Francis George, OMI, and has been authorized for publication by the undersigned.

Msgr. William P. Fay
General Secretary, USCCB

Cover image: Getty Images.

Excerpts from the English translation of *Holy Communion and Worship Outside Mass* © 1974, International Committee on English in the Liturgy, Inc. (ICEL); excerpts from the English translation of *Documents on the Liturgy, 1963-1979: Conciliar, Papal, and Curial Texts* © 1982, ICEL. All rights reserved.

ISBN 978-1-57455-595-0

First Printing, October 2004
Fourth Printing, July 2019

Table of Contents

Introduction

In his encyclical letter *Ecclesia de Eucharistia*, Pope John Paul II speaks of the ways in which the liturgical reform of the Second Vatican Council has led all the faithful "to a more conscious, active and fruitful participation in the Holy Sacrifice of the Altar."[1] Among the liturgical practices that have fostered this participation is adoration of the Most Blessed Sacrament, which can serve as "an inexhaustible source of holiness."[2]

Yet, as the Holy Father sadly notes, "in some places the practice of Eucharistic adoration has been almost completely abandoned," and "in various parts of the Church abuses have occurred, leading to confusion with regard to sound faith and Catholic doctrine concerning this wonderful sacrament."[3]

In the smallest mission and in the grandest basilica, the Church gathers to worship Christ, who feeds us with his own Body and Blood and continues to nourish us with his perduring presence under the species of bread and wine. This brief resource is intended to help bishops, pastors, liturgy committees, and liturgical ministers to better understand the liturgy that the Church prescribes for adoration of the Holy Eucharist.

These pages invite you to listen to the reflections of the bishops of the Committee on the Liturgy on thirty one ritual questions that are frequently encountered by those who plan adoration of the Blessed Sacrament. Excerpts from the liturgical

---

1   Pope John Paul II, *Ecclesia de Eucharistia* (EE) (April 17, 2003) (Washington, DC: USCCB, 2003), no. 10.
2   EE, no. 10.
3   EE, no. 10.

book *Holy Communion and Worship of the Eucharist Outside Mass* describing the liturgy to be followed for the adoration of the Blessed Sacrament are then provided, so that you may read first hand the official liturgical rites that the Church prescribes for such celebrations.

Pope John Paul II has proclaimed October 2004 to October 2005 as the Year of the Eucharist. May we strive ever more fervently to lead all men and women to Christ, present for them in this Holy and Living Sacrifice. In your parish, then, may the Holy Father's words announcing the Eucharistic Year ring true:

> Grateful for this immense gift, [the Church's] members gather round the Blessed Sacrament, for that is the source and summit of her being and action. *Ecclesia de Eucharistia vivit!* The Church draws her life from the Eucharist and knows that this truth does not simply express a daily experience of faith, but recapitulates the heart of the mystery in which she consists.[4]

Monsignor James P. Moroney
Executive Director
USCCB Secretariat for the Liturgy

---

4   Pope John Paul II, homily for the Solemnity of the Body and Blood of Christ (Corpus Christi), June 10, 2004, no. 4, http://www.vatican.va (accessed August 2004).

Thirty-One Questions on Adoration of the Blessed Sacrament

A. WHY HAVE EUCHARISTIC ADORATION?

1. If the Mass is the source and summit of the entire Christian life, then why have Eucharistic adoration?

The celebration of the Most Holy Eucharist is, certainly, the "fount and apex" of the entire Christian life.[1] Yet the "spiritual life . . . is not limited solely to participation in the liturgy."[2] Pope John Paul II calls worship of the Most Holy Eucharist outside Mass "an important daily practice [that] becomes an inexhaustible source of holiness"[3] and a practice "of inestimable value for the life of the Church," so much so that " it is the responsibility of Pastors to encourage, also by their personal witness, the practice of Eucharistic adoration, and exposition of the Blessed Sacrament in particular, as well as prayer of adoration before Christ present under the Eucharistic species."[4]

---

1   Second Vatican Council, *Lumen gentium* (*Dogmatic Constitution on the Church*), no. 11, http://www.vatican.va (accessed August 2004). See *Catechism of the Catholic Church* (CCC), 2nd. ed. (Washington, DC: Libreria Editrice Vaticana–USCCB, 2000), no. 1324.

2   Second Vatican Council, *Sacrosanctum concilium* (*Constitution on the Sacred Liturgy*), (December 4, 1963), no. 12, http://www.vatican.va (accessed August 2004).

3   EE, no. 10; see also Congregation for Divine Worship and the Discipline of the Sacraments, Instruction *Redemptionis Sacramentum* (RS) (*Instruction on the Eucharist*), (March 25, 2004) (Washington, DC: USCCB, 2004), no. 134.

4   EE, no. 25.

2. What is the relationship of Eucharistic adoration to the Mass?

The celebration of the Eucharist in the sacrifice of the Mass is "truly the origin and purpose of the worship that is shown to the Eucharist outside Mass."[5] Eucharistic adoration extends Holy Communion in a lasting way[6] and prepares us to participate more fully in the celebration of the Eucharistic mystery. It leads us to "acknowledge Christ's marvelous presence in the sacrament" and "invites us to the spiritual union with him that culminates in sacramental communion."[7]

3. What is the importance of Eucharistic devotion?

"This practice, repeatedly praised and recommended by the Magisterium, is supported by the example of many saints. Particularly outstanding in this regard was Saint Alphonsus Liguori, who wrote: 'Of all devotions, that of adoring Jesus in the Blessed Sacrament is the greatest after the sacraments, the one dearest to God and the one most helpful to us.' The Eucharist is a priceless treasure: by not only celebrating it but also by praying before it outside of Mass we are enabled to make contact with the very wellspring of grace."[8]

---

5   See Sacred Congregation for Rites, *Eucharisticum mysterium* (EM) (*On the Worship of the Eucharist*) (May 25, 1967), no. 3e, in *Documents on the Liturgy 1963-1979: Conciliar, Papal, and Curial Texts* (Collegeville, MN: Liturgical Press).

6   See Letter of Pope John Paul II to Bishop Albert Houssiau of Liege, Belgium, on the 750th anniversary of the first celebration of the feast of Corpus Christi (May 28, 1996), http://www.vatican.va (accessed August 2004).

7   International Commission on English in the Liturgy (ICEL), trans., *Holy Communion and Worship of the Eucharist Outside Mass* (HCW) (June 21, 1973) (New York: Catholic Book Publishing, 1976), no. 82.

8   *Visite al SS. Sacramento e a Maria Santissima*, Introduction: Opere Ascetiche, Avellino (2000), 295, as cited in EE, no. 25.

4. What happens as we contemplate the presence of Christ in the Blessed Sacrament?

When we contemplate Christ present in the Blessed Sacrament we are given the opportunity to thank him for his passion, death, and glorious resurrection, the marvelous saving act that brought about our redemption. Christ draws near to us, more intimate with us than we are with ourselves. He strengthens our share in his divine life, the life that transforms us into his likeness and, in the Spirit, he gives us access to the Father. As Pope John Paul II reflected in his recent encyclical letter:

> It is pleasant to spend time with him, to lie close to his breast like the Beloved Disciple (cf. Jn 13:25) and to feel the infinite love present in his heart. If in our time Christians must be distinguished above all by the 'art of prayer,' how can we not feel a renewed need to spend time in spiritual converse, in silent adoration, in heartfelt love before Christ present in the Most Holy Sacrament? How often, dear brother and sisters, have I experienced this, and drawn from it strength, consolation and support![9]

5. Why is the Blessed Sacrament reserved in a tabernacle in every Catholic Church?

"The tabernacle was first intended for the reservation of the Eucharist in a worthy place so that it could be brought to the sick and those absent, outside of Mass. As faith in the real presence of Christ in his Eucharist deepened, the Church became conscious of the meaning of silent adoration of the Lord present under the Eucharistic species."[10]

---

9   EE, no. 25.
10   CCC, no. 139; see RS, no. 129.

6. What significance does this reservation of the Eucharist have for the life of Catholics?

"Eucharist is reserved in churches or oratories to serve as the spiritual center of a religious community or a parish community, indeed of the whole Church and the whole of mankind, since it contains, beneath the veil of the species, Christ the invisible Head of the Church, the Redeemer of the world, the center of all hearts, 'by whom all things are and by whom we exist.'"[11] "He is in the midst of us day and night; He dwells in us with the fullness of grace and of truth. He raises the level of morals, fosters virtue, comforts the sorrowful, strengthens the weak and stirs up all those who draw near to Him to imitate Him, so that they may learn from his example to be meek and humble of heart, and to seek not their own interests but those of God."[12]

7. What is the social aspect of Eucharistic adoration?

"Devotion to the divine Eucharist exerts a great influence upon the soul in the direction of fostering a 'social' love, in which we put the common good ahead of private good, take up the cause of the community, the parish, the universal Church, and extend our charity to the whole world because we know that there are members of Christ everywhere. . . . This zeal at prayer and at devoting oneself to God for the sake of the unity of the Church is something that religious, both men and women, should regard as very specially their own since they are bound in a special way to adoration of the Blessed Sacrament, and they have, by virtue of the vows they

---

11   Pope Paul VI, *Mysterium Fidei* (MF) (*On the Mystery of Faith*) (September 3, 1965), no. 68, http://www.vatican.va (accessed September 2004).

12   MF, no. 67.

4

have pronounced, become a kind of crown set around it here on earth."[13]

8. Should priests encourage the faithful to pray before the Blessed Sacrament?

Pope Paul VI urged that the faithful "should not forget about paying a visit during the day to the Most Blessed Sacrament in the very special place of honor where it is reserved in churches in keeping with the liturgical laws, since this is a proof of gratitude and a pledge of love and a display of the adoration that is owed to Christ the Lord who is present there."[14] "Pastors should see that churches and public oratories where, according to law, the holy Eucharist is reserved, are open every day at least for some hours, at a convenient time, so that the faithful may easily pray in the presence of the Blessed Sacrament."[15]

B. THE EXPOSITION OF THE BLESSED SACRAMENT

9. What is the difference between Eucharistic adoration and Eucharistic exposition?

Eucharistic adoration is prayer before the Blessed Sacrament housed within the tabernacle. Eucharistic exposition is the ritual by which the Blessed Sacrament is displayed outside the tabernacle in a monstrance or ciborium for public veneration by the faithful. It is a public celebration that enables the faithful to perceive more clearly the relationship between the reserved Sacrament and the "sacrifice of the Mass [which] is

---

13   MF, nos. 69, 71.
14   MF, no. 66.
15   HCW, no. 8; see *Code of Canon Law* (CIC) (Washington, DC: Canon Law Society of America, 1983), canon 937; see also RS, no. 135.

truly the origin and the purpose of the worship that is shown to the Eucharist outside Mass."[16]

10. What is the purpose of exposition of the Blessed Sacrament?

There are three purposes of Eucharistic exposition: "to acknowledge Christ's marvelous presence in the sacrament,"[17] to lead us to a fuller participation in the celebration of the Eucharist, culminating in Holy Communion,[18] and to foster "the worship which is due to Christ in spirit and in truth."[19]

11. Is the Holy Eucharist exposed for the purpose of private devotion?

No. The liturgical rites for Exposition of the Blessed Sacrament are found in the ritual book *Holy Communion and Worship of the Eucharist Outside of Mass* and presume the presence of a number of people during the period of adoration.[20] The rites require that during the period of exposition "there should be prayers, songs, and readings to direct the attention of the faithful to the worship of Christ the Lord."[21] The Liturgy of the Hours may also be celebrated during the period of exposition,[22] or the Rosary may be prayed.[23]

---

16   EM, no. 3e.
17   HCW, no. 82.
18   See HCW, no. 82.
19   HCW, no. 82.
20   The communal dimension of worship of the exposed Blessed Sacrament is emphasized by the *Code of Canon Law*, canon 942, which requires that annual solemn exposition of the Most Blessed Sacrament "is to be held . . . only if a suitable gathering of the faithful is foreseen and the established norms are observed."
21   HCW, no. 95.
22   See HCW, no. 96.
23   Congregation for Divine Worship and the Discipline of the Sacraments, "Notes on Recitation of the Rosary During Exposition of the Blessed Sacrament," (January 1,

12. How often should adoration of the exposed Blessed Sacrament occur?

"It is recommended that in . . . churches and oratories [where the Eucharist is regularly reserved] an annual solemn exposition of the Most Blessed Sacrament be held for an appropriate period of time, even if not continuous, so that the local community more profoundly meditates on and adores the eucharistic mystery."[24] Thus, every pastor should arrange annually for solemn exposition and adoration of the Blessed Sacrament.

13. What forms might such Solemn Exposition take?

In many places, this exposition takes place for a period of "forty hours," during which the faithful join with local clergy in a continuous period of prayer for forty hours. In other places, shorter periods of continuous prayer before the exposed Blessed Sacrament take place, accompanied by appropriate sacred songs, readings from Scripture, and other forms of liturgical prayer.

14. When the Blessed Sacrament is exposed, how many candles should be used?

"For exposition of the Blessed Sacrament in the monstrance, four to six candles are lighted, as at Mass, and incense is used. For exposition of the Blessed Sacrament in the ciborium, at least two candles should be lighted, and incense may be used."[25]

1998), Prot. no. 2287/96/L, in *BCL Newsletter* 35 (January/February 1999): 62-64; see RS, no. 137.

24   CIC, canon 942; see HCW, no. 86; see also RS, no.139.

25   HCW, no. 85.

15. May Extraordinary Ministers of Holy Communion be deputed to expose the Blessed Sacrament for adoration?

Yes, "such ministers may open the tabernacle and also, if suitable, place the ciborium on the altar or place the host in the monstrance. At the end of the period of adoration, they replace the Blessed Sacrament in the tabernacle. It is not lawful, however, for them to give the blessing with the sacrament."[26]

16. How is the Blessed Sacrament reverenced? How is the reverence different when the Blessed Sacrament is exposed?

What distinguishes the reverence given to the exposed Sacrament from adoration before the tabernacle is the communal nature of reverence to the exposed Sacrament. In Eucharistic exposition, the Blessed Sacrament is reverenced by the common prayer of the people in silence, song, and meditation, by incensation, and by other liturgical acts, including genuflection. "A single genuflection is made in the presence of the Blessed Sacrament, whether reserved in the tabernacle or exposed for public adoration."[27]

17. Can Mass and exposition take place at the same time?

"During the exposition of the Blessed Sacrament, the celebration of Mass is prohibited in the body of the Church. . . . the celebration of the Eucharistic mystery includes in a more perfect

---

26   HCW, no. 91.
27   HCW, no. 84.

way the internal communion to which exposition seeks to lead the faithful."[28]

18. Couldn't the Eucharist be exposed always by building tabernacles of glass or tabernacles with small windows to see inside?

No. "The holy Eucharist is to be reserved in a solid tabernacle. It must be opaque and unbreakable."[29]

C. PERPETUAL ADORATION OF THE EXPOSED BLESSED SACRAMENT

19. What is the difference between perpetual adoration and perpetual exposition of the Blessed Sacrament?

The Blessed Sacrament may be adored while contained in the tabernacle for an extended period of time; this is called "perpetual adoration." Perpetual exposition of the Blessed Sacrament is a liturgical act whereby the consecrated host is placed in a ciborium or in a monstrance outside of the tabernacle for an extended period of time so that the faithful may gather together to pray before the exposed Eucharist.

20. Who regulates the practice of perpetual exposition?

"The local Ordinary has the responsibility for the regulation of perpetual exposition. He determines when it is permissible

---

28   HCW, no. 83; see RS, no. 140.
29   HCW, no. 10.

and establishes the regulations to be followed in regard to perpetual exposition of the Blessed Sacrament."[30]

21. When and where should perpetual exposition of the Blessed Sacrament take place?

Speaking at the forty-fifth International Eucharistic Congress held in Seville, Spain, in June 1993, Pope John Paul II expressed his hope that "in all parishes and Christian communities, there would be established some form of ongoing adoration of the most Blessed Sacrament."[31] Whether this adoration takes the form of perpetual exposition of the Blessed Sacrament is at the discretion of the diocesan bishop.

22. When the bishop approves perpetual adoration of the exposed Blessed Sacrament in a parish Church, where should adoration take place?

Regular or even extended adoration of the Blessed Sacrament may take place in the main body of the Church or in a separate chapel. Perpetual adoration of the exposed Blessed Sacrament should, ordinarily, take place "in a chapel distinct from the body of the church so as not to interfere with the normal activities of the parish or its daily liturgical celebrations."[32]

---

30 Congregation for Divine Worship and the Discipline of the Sacraments, *Responsum ad dubium* received by the USCCB Committee on the Liturgy (July 1995), in *Solemn Exposition of the Holy Eucharist*, Liturgy Documentary Series 11 (Washington, DC: USCCB, 1996), 37.

31 Pope John Paul II, *El Misterio Total de la Eucaristia*, in *Notitiae* 29: 400.

32 *Responsum ad dubium* submitted by the Bishops' Committee on the Liturgy (July 1995), in *Solemn Exposition of the Holy Eucharist*, 36.

23. What should be done when Mass is celebrated in the course of perpetual adoration?

When Mass is celebrated in a chapel where the Blessed Sacrament is exposed, the Eucharist must be replaced in the tabernacle before the celebration of Mass begins.[33] Perpetual exposition is not allowed, however, when such reposition takes place more than twice a day.[34]

24. In those places where perpetual adoration of the exposed Blessed Sacrament take place, scheduling is often a great challenge. If a person misses an assigned hour for adoration of the exposed Sacrament, can a door or a drape be erected so that the exposed Sacrament can be temporarily closed off from public view?

No. The use of drapes or doors to shield the monstrance, even for a short period of time, is not the required reposition of the Blessed Sacrament. The Blessed Sacrament may never be left exposed when no one is present for prayer and adoration. "Every effort should be made to ensure that there should be at least two people present. There must absolutely never be periods when the Blessed Sacrament is exposed and there is no one present for adoration. . . ."[35] "If a period of uninterrupted exposition is not possible, because of too few worshipers, the Blessed Sacrament may be replaced in the tabernacle during

---

33   See HCW, no. 83.

34   See HCW, no. 88.

35   *Responsum ad dubium* received by the USCCB Committee on the Liturgy (July 1995), in *Solemn Exposition of the Holy Eucharist*, 37.

periods which have been scheduled and announced before-hand. This reposition may not take place more often than twice during the day, for example, about noon and at night."[36]

25. In order to enhance security, may the Blessed Sacrament be exposed behind a glass window?

No. The Blessed Sacrament may be exposed in either a mon-strance or ciborium and is usually placed on the altar for ado-ration. The exposition of the Blessed Sacrament behind a glass window is not the "exposition" envisioned by the rite. Such arrangements often result in the appearance of a "glass tabernacle," which is forbidden.

26. Must a perpetual adoration chapel be closed during the Easter Triduum?

"Groups authorized to have perpetual exposition are bound to follow all the liturgical norms given in *Holy Communion and Worship of the Eucharist Outside Mass*, nos. 82-100. Under no circumstances may perpetual exposition take place during the Easter Triduum."[37]

27. May the Rosary be prayed during Eucharistic adoration?

Yes. The Rosary, "a prayer inspired by the Gospel and centered on the mystery of the Incarnation and the Redemption,"

---

36   HCW, no. 88.
37   *Responsum ad dubium* received by the Bishops' Committee on the Liturgy (July 1995), in *Solemn Exposition of the Holy Eucharist*, 36-37.

"should be considered a prayer of deep Christological orientation"[38] and may rightly be counted among the prayers designed to "direct the attention of the faithful to the worship of Christ the Lord."[39] This is especially true if each mystery of the rosary is accompanied by a scriptural or catechetical text emphasizing the Christological orientation of the mystery. In any case, the recitation of the Rosary before the exposed Sacrament should help lead the faithful back "to a knowledge and love of the Lord Jesus, to union with him, finding great encouragement and support in liturgical prayer before the Eucharist."[40]

D. EUCHARISTIC ADORATION AFTER THE MASS OF THE LORD'S SUPPER ON HOLY THURSDAY

28. What is the purpose of Eucharistic Adoration after the Mass of the Lord's Supper on Holy Thursday?

If the Liturgy of the Lord's Passion is to be celebrated the next day, the Blessed Sacrament is solemnly reserved in a separate repository at the end of the Evening Mass of the Lord's Supper. While the primary purpose of this reservation is to provide the "eucharistic bread that will be distributed in communion on

---

38 Pope Paul VI, *Marialis Cultus* (*For the Right Ordering and Development of Devotion to the Blessed Virgin Mary*), no. 46, cited in Congregation for Divine Worship and the Discipline of the Sacraments, "Notes on Recitation of the Rosary During Exposition of the Blessed Sacrament" (January 1, 1998), Prot. no. 2287/96/L, in *BCL Newsletter* 35 (January/February 1999): 62-64.

39 HCW, no. 95.

40 Congregation for Divine Worship and the Discipline of the Sacraments, "Notes on Recitation of the Rosary During Exposition of the Blessed Sacrament," in *BCL Newsletter* 35: 62-64; see also RS, no. 137.

Good Friday,"[41] the adoration also serves as extension of the Eucharistic liturgy and an acknowledgement of the perduring presence of Christ in the Holy Eucharist.

29. How long should adoration of the Blessed Sacrament last on Holy Thursday night?

"After the Mass of the Lord's Supper, the faithful should be encouraged to spend a suitable period of time during the night in the church in adoration before the Blessed Sacrament that has been solemnly reserved. . . . From midnight onward, however, the adoration should be made without external solemnity, for the day of the Lord's passion has begun."[42]

30. Can the Blessed Sacrament be exposed in a monstrance or ciborium at the repository?

No. "The Blessed Sacrament should be reserved in a closed tabernacle or pyx. Under no circumstances may it be exposed in a monstrance."[43]

31. Is the adoration to take place in silence?

While this adoration is usually characterized by silent prayer, "where appropriate, this prolonged eucharistic adoration may be accompanied by the reading of some part of the Gospel of Saint John (ch. 13-17)."[44]

---

41 Congregation for Divine Worship, *Circular Letter Concerning the Preparation and Celebration of the Easter Feasts* (EF) (January 16, 1988) (Washington, DC: USCCB, 1988), no. 55.

42 EF, no. 56.

43 EF, no. 55.

44 EF, no. 56.

APPENDIX A

Excerpts from

Instruction on the Eucharist
Redemptionis Sacramentum

*On Certain Matters to Be Observed or
to Be Avoided Regarding the Most Holy Eucharist*

From Congregation for Divine Worship and the Discipline of the Sacraments. *Instruction on the Eucharist* (*Redemptionis Sacramentum*). Liturgy Documentary Series 15. Washington, DC: United States Conference of Catholic Bishops, 2004.

CHAPTER VI

The Reservation of the Most Holy Eucharist and Eucharistic Worship Outside Mass

1. THE RESERVATION OF THE MOST HOLY EUCHARIST

129. "The celebration of the Eucharist in the Sacrifice of the Mass is truly the origin and end of the worship given to the Eucharist outside the Mass. Furthermore the sacred species are reserved after Mass principally so that the faithful who cannot be present at Mass, above all the sick and those advanced in age, may be united by sacramental Communion to Christ and his Sacrifice which is offered in the Mass."[219] In addition, this reservation also permits the practice of adoring this great Sacrament and offering it the worship due to God. Accordingly, forms of adoration that are not only private but also public and communitarian in nature, as established or approved by the Church herself, must be greatly promoted.[220]

130. "According to the structure of each church building and in accordance with legitimate local customs, the Most Holy Sacrament is to be reserved in a tabernacle in a part of the church that is noble, prominent, readily visible, and adorned

---

219 S. Congregation for Divine Worship, Decree, *Eucharistiae sacramentum*, 21 June 1973: AAS 65 (1973) p. 610.
220 Cf. ibid.

in a dignified manner" and furthermore "suitable for prayer" by reason of the quietness of the location, the space available in front of the tabernacle, and also the supply of benches or seats and kneelers.[221] In addition, diligent attention should be paid to all the prescriptions of the liturgical books and to the norm of law,[222] especially as regards the avoidance of the danger of profanation.[223]

131. Apart from the prescriptions of canon 934 §1, it is forbidden to reserve the Blessed Sacrament in a place that is not subject in a secure way to the authority of the diocesan Bishop, or where there is a danger of profanation. Where such is the case, the diocesan Bishop should immediately revoke any permission for reservation of the Eucharist that may already have been granted.[224]

132. No one may carry the Most Holy Eucharist to his or her home, or to any other place contrary to the norm of law. It should also be borne in mind that removing or retaining the consecrated species for a sacrilegious purpose or casting them away are *graviora delicta*, the absolution of which is reserved to the Congregation for the Doctrine of the Faith.[225]

---

221 Cf. S. Congregation of Rites, Instruction, *Eucharisticum mysterium*, no. 54: AAS 59 (1967) p. 568; Instruction, *Inter Oecumenici*, 26 September 1964, no. 95: AAS 56 (1964) pp. 877-900, here p. 898; Missale Romanum, *Institutio Generalis*, no. 314.

222 Cf. Pope John Paul II, Letter, *Dominicae Cenae*, no. 3: AAS 72 (1980) pp. 117-119; S. Congregation of Rites, Instruction, *Eucharisticum mysterium*, no. 53: AAS 59 (1967) p. 568; *Code of Canon Law*, can. 938 §2; Roman Ritual, *Holy Communion and Worship of the Eucharist Outside Mass*, Introduction, no. 9; Missale Romanum, *Institutio Generalis*, nos. 314-317.

223 Cf. *Code of Canon Law*, can. 938 §§3-5.

224 S. Congregation for the Discipline of the Sacraments, Instruction, *Nullo unquam*, 26 May 1938, no. 10d: AAS 30 (1938) pp. 198-207, here p. 206.

225 Cf. Pope John Paul II, Apostolic Letter (Motu Proprio), *Sacramentorum sanctitatis tutela*, 30 April 2001: AAS 93 (2001) pp. 737-739; Congregation for the Doctrine of the Faith, *Ep. ad totius Catholicae Ecclesiae Episcopos aliosque Ordinarios et Hierarchas quorum interest: De delictis gravioribus eidem Congregationi pro Doctrina Fidei reservatis*: AAS 93 (2001) p. 786.

133. A Priest or Deacon, or an extraordinary minister who takes the Most Holy Eucharist when an ordained minister is absent or impeded in order to administer it as Communion for a sick person, should go insofar as possible directly from the place where the Sacrament is reserved to the sick person's home, leaving aside any profane business so that any danger of profanation may be avoided and the greatest reverence for the Body of Christ may be ensured. Furthermore the Rite for the administration of Communion to the sick, as prescribed in the Roman Ritual, is always to be used.[226]

2. CERTAIN FORMS OF WORSHIP OF THE MOST HOLY EUCHARIST OUTSIDE MASS

134. "The worship of the Eucharist outside the Sacrifice of the Mass is a tribute of inestimable value in the life of the Church. Such worship is closely linked to the celebration of the Eucharistic Sacrifice."[227] Therefore both public and private devotion to the Most Holy Eucharist even outside Mass should be vigorously promoted, for by means of it the faithful give adoration to Christ, truly and really present,[228] the "High Priest of the good things to come"[229] and Redeemer of the

---

226 Cf. Roman Ritual, *Holy Communion and Worship of the Eucharist Outside Mass*, nos. 26-78.

227 Pope John Paul II, Encyclical Letter, *Ecclesia de Eucharistia*, no. 25: AAS 95 (2003) pp. 449-450.

228 Cf. Ecumenical Council of Trent, Session XIII, 11 October 1551, *Decree on the Most Holy Eucharist*, Chapter 5: DS 1643; Pope Pius XII, Encyclical Letter, *Mediator Dei*: AAS 39 (1947) p. 569; Pope Paul VI, Encyclical Letter, *Mysterium Fidei*, 3 September

228 1965: AAS 57 (1965) pp. 751-774, here pp. 769-770; S. Congregation of Rites, Instruction, *Eucharisticum mysterium*, no. 3f: AAS 59 (1967) p. 543; S. Congregation for the Sacraments and Divine Worship, Instruction, *Inaestimabile donum*, no. 20: AAS 72 (1980) p. 339; Pope John Paul II, Encyclical Letter, *Ecclesia de Eucharistia*, no. 25: AAS 95 (2003) pp. 449-450.

229 Cf. Heb 9:11; Pope John Paul II, Encyclical Letter, *Ecclesia de Eucharistia*, no. 3: AAS 95 (2003) p. 435.

whole world. "It is the responsibility of sacred Pastors, even by the witness of their life, to support the practice of Eucharistic worship and especially exposition of the Most Holy Sacrament, as well as prayer of adoration before Christ present under the eucharistic species."[230]

135. The faithful "should not omit making visits during the day to the Most Holy Sacrament, as a proof of gratitude, a pledge of love, and a debt of the adoration due to Christ the Lord who is present in it."[231] For the contemplation of Jesus present in the Most Holy Sacrament, as a communion of desire, powerfully joins the faithful to Christ, as is splendidly evident in the example of so many Saints.[232] "Unless there is a grave reason to the contrary, a church in which the Most Holy Eucharist is reserved should be open to the faithful for at least some hours each day, so that they can spend time in prayer before the Most Holy Sacrament."[233]

136. The Ordinary should diligently foster Eucharistic adoration, whether brief or prolonged or almost continuous, with the participation of the people. For in recent years in so many places "adoration of the Most Holy Sacrament is also an important daily practice and becomes an inexhaustible source of holiness," although there are also places "where there is evident almost a total lack of regard for worship in the form of eucharistic adoration."[234]

---

230 Pope John Paul II, Encyclical Letter, *Ecclesia de Eucharistia*, no. 25: AAS 95 (2003) p. 450.
231 Pope Paul VI, Encyclical Letter, *Mysterium fidei*: AAS 57 (1965) p. 771.
232 Cf. Pope John Paul II, Encyclical Letter, *Ecclesia de Eucharistia*, no. 25: AAS 95 (2003) pp. 449-450.
233 *Code of Canon Law*, can. 937.
234 Pope John Paul II, Encyclical Letter, *Ecclesia de Eucharistia*, no. 10: AAS 95 (2003) p. 439.

137. Exposition of the Most Holy Eucharist must always be carried out in accordance with the prescriptions of the liturgical books.[235] Before the Most Holy Sacrament either reserved or exposed, the praying of the Rosary, which is admirable "in its simplicity and even its profundity," is not to be excluded either.[236] Even so, especially if there is Exposition, the character of this kind of prayer as a contemplation of the mystery of the life of Christ the Redeemer and the Almighty Father's design of salvation should be emphasized, especially by making use of readings taken from Sacred Scripture.[237]

138. Still, the Most Holy Sacrament, when exposed, must never be left unattended even for the briefest space of time. It should therefore be arranged that at least some of the faithful always be present at fixed times, even if they take alternating turns.

139. Where the diocesan Bishop has sacred ministers or others whom he can assign to this purpose, the faithful have a right to visit the Most Holy Sacrament of the Eucharist frequently for adoration, and to take part in adoration before the Most Holy Eucharist exposed at least at some time in the course of any given year.

140. It is highly recommended that at least in the cities and the larger towns the diocesan Bishop should designate a church building for perpetual adoration; in it, however, Holy Mass should be celebrated frequently, even daily if possible, while

235   Cf. Roman Ritual, *Holy Communion and Worship of the Eucharist Outside Mass*, nos. 82-100; Missale Romanum, *Institutio Generalis*, no. 317; *Code of Canon Law*, can. 941 §2.
236   Pope John Paul II, Apostolic Letter, *Rosarium Virginis Mariae*, 16 October 2002: AAS 95 (2003) pp. 5-36, here no. 2, p. 6.
237   Cf. Congregation for Divine Worship and the Discipline of the Sacraments, Letter of the Congregation, 15 January 1997: *Notitiae* 34 (1998) pp. 506-510; Apostolic Penitentiary, Letter to a Priest, 8 March 1996: *Notitiae* 34 (1998) p. 511.

the Exposition should rigorously be interrupted while Mass is being celebrated.[238] It is fitting that the host to be exposed for adoration should be consecrated in the Mass immediately preceding the time of adoration, and that it should be placed in the monstrance upon the altar after Communion.[239]

141. The diocesan Bishop should acknowledge and foster insofar as possible the right of the various groups of Christ's faithful to form guilds or associations for the carrying out of adoration, even almost continuous adoration. Whenever such associations assume an international character, it pertains to the Congregation for Divine Worship and the Discipline of the Sacraments to erect them and to approve their statutes.[240]

3. EUCHARISTIC CONGRESSES AND EUCHARISTIC PROCESSIONS

142. "It is for the diocesan Bishop to establish regulations about processions in order to provide for participation in them and for their being carried out in a dignified way"[241] and to promote adoration by the faithful.

143. "Wherever it is possible in the judgment of the diocesan Bishop, a procession through the public streets should be held,

---

238 Cf. S. Congregation of Rites, Instruction, *Eucharisticum mysterium*, no. 61: AAS 59 (1967) p. 571; Roman Ritual, *Holy Communion and Worship of the Eucharist Outside Mass*, no. 83; Missale Romanum, *Institutio Generalis*, no. 317; *Code of Canon Law*, can. 941 §2.

239 Cf. Roman Ritual, *Holy Communion and Worship of the Eucharist Outside Mass*, no. 94.

240 Cf. Pope John Paul II, Apostolic Constitution, *Pastor bonus*, article 65: AAS 80 (1988) p. 877.

241 *Code of Canon Law*, can. 944 §2; cf. Roman Ritual, *Holy Communion and Worship of the Eucharist Outside Mass*, Introduction, no. 102; Missale Romanum, *Institutio Generalis*, no. 317.

especially on the Solemnity of the Body and Blood of Christ as a public witness of reverence for the Most Holy Sacrament,"[242] for the "devout participation of the faithful in the eucharistic procession on the Solemnity of the Body and Blood of Christ is a grace from the Lord which yearly fills with joy those who take part in it."[243]

144. Although this cannot be done in some places, the tradition of holding Eucharistic processions should not be allowed to be lost. Instead, new ways should be sought of holding them in today's conditions: for example, at shrines, or in public gardens if the civil authority agrees.

145. The pastoral value of Eucharistic Congresses should be highly esteemed, and they "should be a genuine sign of faith and charity."[244] Let them be diligently prepared and carried out in accordance with what has been laid down,[245] so that Christ's faithful may have the occasion to worship the sacred mysteries of the Body and Blood of the Son of God in a worthy manner, and that they may continually experience within themselves the fruits of the Redemption.[246]

---

242 *Code of Canon Law*, can. 944 §1; cf. Roman Ritual, *Holy Communion and Worship of the Eucharist Outside Mass*, Introduction, nos. 101-102; Missale Romanum, *Institutio Generalis*, no. 317.

243 Pope John Paul II, Encyclical Letter, *Ecclesia de Eucharistia*, no. 10: AAS 95 (2003) p. 439.

244 Cf. Roman Ritual, *Holy Communion and Worship of the Eucharist Outside Mass*, Introduction, no. 109.

245 Cf. ibid., nos. 109-112.

246 Cf. Missale Romanum, *In sollemnitate sanctissimi Corporis et Sanguinis Christi, Collecta*, p. 489.

APPENDIX B

Excerpts from

Holy Communion and Worship of the Eucharist Outside Mass

Holy Communion and Worship of the Eucharist Outside Mass is the English-language vernacular edition of De Sacra Communione et de Cultu Mysterii Eucharistici Extra Missam. It contains the only authorized Roman Catholic liturgical rites for adoration of the Blessed Sacrament.

Reprinted from Holy Communion and Worship of the Eucharist Outside Mass. Translated by International Commission on English in the Liturgy. New York: Catholic Book Publishing, 1976.

General Introduction

I. THE RELATIONSHIP BETWEEN EUCHARISTIC WORSHIP OUTSIDE MASS AND THE EUCHARISTIC CELEBRATION

1. The celebration of the Eucharist is the center of the entire Christian life, both for the Church universal and for the local congregations of the Church. "The other sacraments, all the ministries of the Church, and the works of the apostolate are united with the Eucharist and are directed toward it. For the holy Eucharist contains the entire spiritual treasure of the Church, that is, Christ himself, our Passover and living bread. Through his flesh, made living and life-giving by the Holy Spirit, he offers life to men, who are thus invited and led to offer themselves, their work, and all creation together with him."[1]

2. "The celebration of the Eucharist in the sacrifice of the Mass," moreover, "is truly the origin and the goal of the worship which is shown to the Eucharist outside Mass."[2] Christ the Lord "is offered in the sacrifice of the Mass when he becomes present sacramentally as the spiritual food of the faithful under the appearance of bread and wine." And, "once the sacrifice is offered and while the Eucharist is reserved in churches and oratories, he is truly Emmanuel, 'God with us.' He is in our midst day and night; full of grace and truth, he dwells among us."[3]

---

1 Second Vatican Council, decree *Presbyterorum ordinis*, no. 5.
2 Congregation of Rites, instruction *Eucharisticum mysterium*, no. 3e: AAS 59 (1967) 542.
3 Ibid., no. 36: loc. cit. 541; Paul VI, encyclical *Mysterium fidei*, near the end: AAS 57 (1965) 771.

3. No one therefore may doubt "that all the faithful show this holy sacrament the veneration and adoration which is due to God himself, as has always been customary in the Catholic Church. Nor is the sacrament to be less the object of adoration because it was instituted by Christ the Lord to be received as food."[4]

4. In order to direct and to encourage devotion to the sacrament of the Eucharist correctly, the Eucharistic mystery must be considered in all its fullness, both in the celebration of Mass and in the worship of the sacrament which is reserved after Mass to extend the grace of the sacrifice.[5]

II. THE PURPOSE OF EUCHARISTIC RESERVATION

5. The primary and original reason for reservation of the Eucharist outside Mass is the administration of viaticum. The secondary reasons are the giving of communion and the adoration of our Lord Jesus Christ who is present in the sacrament. The reservation of the sacrament for the sick led to the praiseworthy practice of adoring this heavenly food in the churches. This cult of adoration rests upon an authentic and solid basis, especially because faith in the real presence of the Lord leads naturally to external, public expression of that faith.[6]

6. In the celebration of Mass the chief ways in which Christ is present in his Church gradually become clear. First he is present in the very assembly of the faithful, gathered together in his name; next he is present his word, when the Scriptures are read

---

4 Congregation of Rites, instruction *Eucharisticum mysterium*, no. 3f: AAS 59 (1967) 543.

5 See ibid., no. 3g: loc. cit. 543.

6 See ibid., no. 49: loc. cit. 566-567.

in the Church and explained; then in the person of the minister; finally and above all, in the Eucharistic sacrament. In a way that is completely unique, the whole and entire Christ, God and man, is substantially and permanently present in the sacrament. This presence of Christ under the appearance of bread and wine "is called real, not to exclude other kinds of presence as if they were not real, but because it is real *par excellence*."[7]

Therefore, to express the sign of the Eucharist, it is more in harmony with the nature of the celebration that, at the altar where Mass is celebrated, there should if possible be no reservation of the sacrament in the tabernacle from the beginning of Mass. The Eucharistic presence of Christ is the fruit of the consecration and should appear to be such.[8]

7. The consecrated hosts are to be frequently renewed and reserved in a ciborium or other vessel, in a number sufficient for the communion of the sick and others outside Mass.[9]

8. Pastors should see that churches and public oratories where, according to law, the holy Eucharist is reserved, are open every day at least for some hours, at a convenient time, so that the faithful may easily pray in the presence of the Blessed Sacrament.

III. THE PLACE OF EUCHARISTIC RESERVATION

9. The place for the reservation of the Eucharist should be truly preeminent. It is highly recommended that the place be

---

7   Paul VI, encyclical *Mysterium fidei*: AAS 57 (1965) 764; see Congregation of Rites, instruction *Eucharisticum mysterium*, no. 55: AAS 59 (1967) 568-569.

8   See Congregation of Rites, instruction *Eucharisticum mysterium*, no. 55: AAS 59 (1967) 568-569.

9   See Roman Missal, *General Instruction*, nos. 285 and 292.

suitable also for private adoration and prayer so that the faithful may easily, fruitfully, and constantly honor the Lord, present in the sacrament, through personal worship.

This will be achieved more easily if the chapel is separate from the body of the church, especially in churches where marriages and funerals are celebrated frequently and churches which are much visited by pilgrims or because of their artistic and historical treasures.[10]

10. The holy Eucharist is to be reserved in a solid tabernacle. It must be opaque and unbreakable. Ordinarily there should be only one tabernacle in a church; this may be placed on an altar or, at the discretion of the local Ordinary, in some other noble and properly ornamented part of the church other than an altar.[11]

The key to the tabernacle where the Eucharist is reserved must be kept most carefully by the priest in charge of the church or oratory or by a special minister who has received the faculty to give communion.

11. The presence of the Eucharist in the tabernacle is to be shown by a veil or in another suitable way determined by the competent authority.

According to traditional usage, an oil lamp or lamp with a wax candle is to burn constantly near the tabernacle as a sign of the honor which is shown to the Lord.[12]

---

10   See Congregation of Rites, instruction *Eucharisticum mysterium*, no. 51: AAS 59 (1967) 567.
11   See ibid., nos. 52-53: loc. cit., 567-568.
12   See ibid., no. 57: loc. cit., 569.

IV. THE COMPETENCE OF
EPISCOPAL CONFERENCES

12. It is for episcopal conferences, in the preparation of particular rituals in accord with the Constitution on the Liturgy (no. 63b), to accommodate this title of the Roman Ritual to the needs of individual regions so that, their actions having been confirmed by the Apostolic See, the ritual may be followed in the respective regions.

In this matter it will be for the conferences:

a. to consider carefully and prudently what elements, if any, of popular traditions may be retained or introduced, provided they can be harmonized with the spirit of the liturgy, and then to propose to the Apostolic See the adaptations they judge necessary or useful; these may be introduced with the consent of the Apostolic See;

b. to prepare translations of texts which are truly accommodated to the character of various languages and the mentality of various cultures; they may add texts, especially for singing, with appropriate melodies.

Liturgical texts, which are used in respect of a man, may be used with a change of gender for a woman also. And in either case the singular may be changed into the plural.

CHAPTER III

Forms of the Worship of the Holy Eucharist

1. EXPOSITION OF THE HOLY EUCHARIST

Introduction

I. Relationship Between Exposition and Mass

82. Exposition of the holy Eucharist, either in the ciborium or in the monstrance, is intended to acknowledge Christ's marvelous presence in the sacrament. Exposition invites us to the spiritual union with him that culminates in sacramental communion. Thus it fosters very well the worship which is due to Christ in spirit and in truth.

This kind of exposition must clearly express the cult of the Blessed Sacrament in its relationship to the Mass. The plan of the exposition should carefully avoid anything which might somehow obscure the principal desire of Christ in instituting the Eucharist, namely, to be with us as food, medicine, and comfort.[4]

83. During the exposition of the Blessed Sacrament, the celebration of Mass is prohibited in the body of the Church. In addition to the reasons given in no. 6, the celebration of the Eucharistic mystery includes in a more perfect way the internal communion to which exposition seeks to lead the faithful.

---

4   See ibid., no. 60: loc. cit., 570.

29

If exposition of the Blessed Sacrament is extended for an entire day or over several days, it is to be interrupted during the celebration of Mass. Mass may be celebrated in a chapel distinct from the area of exposition if at least some members of the faithful remain in adoration.[5]

II. Regulations for Exposition

84. A single genuflection is made in the presence of the Blessed Sacrament, whether reserved in the tabernacle or exposed for public adoration.

85. For exposition of the Blessed Sacrament in the monstrance, four to six candles are lighted, as at Mass, and incense is used. For exposition of the Blessed Sacrament in the ciborium, at least two candles should be lighted, and incense may be used.

LENGTHY EXPOSITION

86. In churches where the Eucharist is regularly reserved, it is recommended that solemn exposition of the Blessed Sacrament for an extended period of time should take place once a year, even though this period is not strictly continuous. In this way the local community may reflect more profoundly upon this mystery and adore Christ in the sacrament.

This kind of exposition, however, may take place, with the consent of the local Ordinary, only if suitable numbers of the faithful are expected to be present.[6]

87. For a grave and general necessity the local Ordinary may direct that a more extended period of supplication before the

---

5   See ibid., no. 61: loc. cit.; 570-571.
6   See ibid., no. 63: loc. cit., 571.

Blessed Sacrament exposed take place in churches where the faithful assemble in large numbers.[7]

88. If a period of uninterrupted exposition is not possible, because of too few worshipers, the Blessed Sacrament may be replaced in the tabernacle during periods which have been scheduled and announced beforehand. This reposition may not take place more often than twice during the day, for example, about noon and at night.

The following form of simple reposition may be observed: the priest or deacon, vested in an alb, or a surplice over a cassock, and a stole, replaces the Blessed Sacrament in the tabernacle after a brief period of adoration and a prayer said with those present. The exposition of the Blessed Sacrament may take place in the same manner (at the scheduled time).[8]

BRIEF PERIOD OF EXPOSITION

89. Shorter expositions of the Eucharist are to be arranged in such a way that the blessing with the Eucharist is preceded by a suitable period for readings of the word of God, songs, prayers, and sufficient time for silent prayer.[9]

Exposition which is held exclusively for the giving of benediction is prohibited.

ADORATION IN RELIGIOUS COMMUNITIES

90. According to the constitutions and regulations of their institute, some religious communities and other groups have the practice of perpetual Eucharistic adoration or adoration over extended periods of time. It is strongly recommended that they pattern this holy practice in harmony with the spirit

---

7   See ibid., no. 64: loc. cit., 572.
8   See ibid., no. 65: loc. cit., 572.
9   See ibid., no. 66: loc. cit., 572.

of the liturgy. Thus, when the whole community takes part in adoration before Christ the Lord, readings, songs, and religious silence may foster effectively the spiritual life of the community. This will promote among the members of the religious house the spirit of unity and brotherhood which the Eucharist signifies and effects, and the cult of the sacrament may express a noble form of worship.

The form of adoration in which one or two members of the community take turns before the Blessed Sacrament is also to be maintained and is highly commended. In accordance with the life of the institute, as approved by the Church, the worshipers adore Christ the Lord in the sacrament and pray to him in the name of the whole community and of the Church.

III. The Minister of Exposition

91. The ordinary minister for exposition of the Eucharist is a priest or deacon. At the end of the period of adoration, before the reposition, he blesses the people with the sacrament.

In the absence of a priest or deacon or if they are lawfully impeded, the following persons may publicly expose and later repose the holy Eucharist for the adoration of the faithful:

- a. an acolyte or special minister of communion;
- b. a member of a religious communion or of a lay association of men or women which is devoted to Eucharistic adoration, upon appointment by the local Ordinary.

Such ministers may open the tabernacle and also, if suitable, place the ciborium on the altar or place the host in the monstrance. At the end of the period of adoration, they replace the Blessed Sacrament in the tabernacle. It is not lawful, however, for them to give the blessing with the sacrament.

92. The minister, if he is a priest or deacon, should vest in an alb, or a surplice over a cassock, and a stole. Other ministers should wear either the liturgical vestments which are used in the region or the vesture which is suitable for this ministry and which has been approved by the Ordinary.

The priest or deacon should wear a white cope and humeral veil to give the blessing at the end of adoration, when the exposition takes place with the monstrance; in the case of exposition in the ciborium, the humeral veil should be worn.

Rite of Eucharistic Exposition and Benediction Exposition

Exposition

93. After the people have assembled, a song may be sung while the minister comes to the altar. If the holy Eucharist is not reserved at the altar where the exposition is to take place, the minister puts on a humeral veil and brings the sacrament from the place of reservation; he is accompanied by servers or by the faithful with lighted candles.

The ciborium or monstrance should be placed upon the table of the altar which is covered with a cloth. If exposition with the monstrance is to extend over a long period, a throne in an elevated position may be used, but this should not be too lofty or distant.[10] After exposition, if the monstrance is used, the minister incenses the sacrament. If the adoration is to be lengthy, he may then withdraw.

---

10   See ibid., no. 62: loc. cit., 571.

94. In the case of more solemn and lengthy exposition, the host should be consecrated in the Mass which immediately precedes the exposition and after communion should be placed in the monstrance upon the altar. The Mass ends with the prayer after communion, and the concluding rites are omitted. Before the priest leaves, he may place the Blessed Sacrament on the throne and incense it.

Adoration

95. During the exposition there should be prayers, songs, and readings to direct the attention of the faithful to the worship of Christ the Lord.

To encourage a prayerful spirit, there should be readings from scripture with a homily or brief exhortations to develop a better understanding of the Eucharistic mystery. It is also desirable for the people to respond to the word of God by singing and to spend some periods of time in religious silence.

96. Part of the liturgy of the hours, especially the principal hours, may be celebrated before the Blessed Sacrament when there is a lengthy period of exposition. This liturgy extends the praise and thanksgiving offered to God in the Eucharistic celebration to the several hours of the day; it directs the prayers of the Church to Christ and through him to the Father in the name of the whole world.

Benediction

97. Toward the end of the exposition the priest or deacon goes to the altar, genuflects, and kneels. Then a hymn or other Eucharistic song is sung.[11] Meanwhile the minister, while

---

11   See below, nos. 192-199.

kneeling, incenses the Sacrament if the exposition has taken place with the monstrance.

98. Afterward the minister rises and sings or says:

Let us pray.

After a brief period of silence, the minister continues:

Lord Jesus Christ,
you gave us the Eucharist
as the memorial of your suffering and death.
May our worship of this sacrament of your body
      and blood
help us to experience the salvation you won for us
and the peace of the kingdom
where you live with the Father and the
      Holy Spirit,
one God, for ever and ever.

All respond:

Amen.

OR:

[224]

Lord our God,
in this great sacrament
we come into the presence of Jesus Christ,
      your Son,
born of the Virgin Mary
and crucified for our salvation.
May we who declare our faith in this fountain of
      love and mercy
drink from it the water of everlasting life.
We ask this through Christ our Lord.

OR:

[225]

Lord our God,
may we always give due honor
to the sacramental presence of the Lamb who
    was slain for us.
May our faith be rewarded
by the vision of his glory,
who lives and reigns for ever and ever.

OR:

[226]

Lord our God,
you have given us the true bread from heaven.
In the strength of this food
may we live always by your life
and rise in glory on the last day.
We ask this through Christ our Lord.

OR:

[227]

Lord,
give to our hearts
the light of faith and the fire of love,
that we may worship in spirit and in truth
our God and Lord, present in this sacrament,
who lives and reigns for ever and ever.

OR:

[228]

Lord,
may this sacrament of new life
warm our hearts with your love

and make us eager
for the eternal joy of your kingdom.
We ask this through Christ our Lord.

OR:

[229]

Lord our God,
teach us to cherish in our hearts
the paschal mystery of your Son
by which you redeemed the world.
Watch over the gifts of grace
your love has given us
and bring them to fulfillment
in the glory of heaven.
We ask this through Christ our Lord.

99. After the prayer the priest or deacon puts on the humeral veil, genuflects, and takes the monstrance or ciborium. He makes the sign of the cross over the people with the monstrance or ciborium, in silence.

Reposition

100. After the blessing the priest or deacon who gave the blessing, or another priest or deacon, replaces the Blessed Sacrament in the tabernacle and genuflects. Meanwhile the people may sing or say an acclamation, and the minister then leaves.

2. EUCHARISTIC PROCESSIONS

101. When the Eucharist is carried through the streets in a solemn procession with singing, the Christian people give public witness of faith and devotion toward the sacrament.

It is for the local Ordinary, however, to judge whether this is opportune in today's circumstances, and to determine the time, place, and order of such processions, so that they may be conducted with dignity and without loss of reverence to the sacrament.[12]

102. The annual procession on the feast of Corpus Christi, or on an appropriate day near this feast, has a special importance and meaning for the pastoral life of the parish or city. It is therefore desirable to continue this procession, in accordance with the law, when today's circumstances permit and when it can truly be a sign of common faith and adoration.

In the principal districts of large cities there may be additional Eucharistic processions for pastoral reasons at the discretion of the local Ordinary. If the procession cannot be held on the feast of Corpus Christi, it is fitting to hold some kind of public celebration for the entire city or its principal districts in the cathedral church or other appropriate places.

103. It is fitting that a Eucharistic procession begin after the Mass in which the host to be carried in the procession has been consecrated. A procession may also take place, however, at the end of a lengthy period of public adoration.

104. Eucharistic processions should be arranged in accordance with local customs concerning the decoration of the streets and the order followed by the participants. In the course of the procession there may be stations where the Eucharistic blessing is given, if this custom is in effect and is of pastoral advantage. Songs and prayers should be so directed that all proclaim their faith in Christ and direct their attention to the Lord alone.

---

12   See Congregation of Rites, instruction *Eucharisticum mysterium*, no. 59: AAS 59 (1967) 570.

105. The priest who carries the Blessed Sacrament may wear the vestments used for the celebration of Mass if the procession takes place immediately afterward, or he may vest in a white cope.

106. Lights, incense, and the canopy under which the priest carrying the Blessed Sacrament walks should be used in accordance with local customs.

107. It is fitting that the procession should go from one church to another. Nevertheless, if local circumstances require, the procession may return to the same church where it began.

108. At the end of the procession benediction with the Blessed Sacrament should be given in the church where the procession ends or at another appropriate place. Then the Blessed Sacrament is reposed.

3. EUCHARISTIC CONGRESSES

109. Eucharistic congresses have been introduced into the life of the Church in recent years as a special manifestation of Eucharistic worship. They should be considered as a kind of station to which a particular community invites an entire local church or to which an individual local church invites other churches of a single region or nation or even of the entire world. The purpose is that together the members of the church join in the deepest profession of some aspect of the Eucharistic mystery and express their worship publicly in the bond of charity and unity.

Such congresses should be a genuine sign of faith and charity by reason of the total participation of the local church and the association with it of the other churches.

110. Both the local church and other churches should under-take studies beforehand concerning the place, theme, and program of the congress. These studies will lead to the consideration of genuine needs and will foster the progress of theological studies and the good of the local church. Specialists in theological, biblical, liturgical, pastoral, and humane studies should help in this research.

111. In preparation for a Eucharistic congress, primary consideration should be given to the following:

a.   a thorough catechesis concerning the Eucharist, especially as the mystery of Christ living and working in the Church, accommodated to the capacity of different groups;

b.   more active participation in the liturgy in order to encourage a religious hearing of the word of God and the spirit of brotherhood and community;[13]

c.   research and promotion of social undertakings for human development and the proper distribution of property, including temporal property, following the example of the primitive Christian community.[14] Thus the ferment of the Gospel, as a force in the growth of contemporary society and as the pledge of the future kingdom,[15] may be diffused in some measure at the Eucharistic table.

---

13   Second Vatican Council, constitution *Sacrosanctum Concilium*, nos. 41-52; constitution *Lumen gentium*, no. 26.

14   See Acts 4:32.

15   Second Vatican Council, constitution *Sacrosanctum Concilium*, no. 47; decree *Unitatis redintegratio*, no. 15.

112. The celebration of the congress should follow these criteria:[16]

   a. the celebration of the Eucharist should be the true center and high point of the congress to which all the efforts and the various devotional services should be directed;

   b. celebrations of the word of God, catechetical meetings, and public conferences should be planned to investigate thoroughly the theme of the congress and to propose clearly the practical aspects to be carried out;

   c. there should be an opportunity for common prayers and extended adoration in the presence of the Blessed Sacrament exposed at designated churches which are especially suited to this form of piety;

   d. the regulations concerning Eucharistic processions[17] should be observed for the procession in which the Blessed Sacrament is carried through the streets of the city with common hymns and prayers, taking into account local, social, and religious conditions.

---

16   See Congregation of Rites, instruction *Eucharisticum mysterium*, no. 67: AAS 59 (1967) 572-573.

17   See above, nos. 101-108.